ALL AROUND THE WORLD
SLOVAKIA

by Kristine Spanier, MLIS

T0014728

pogo

Ideas for Parents and Teachers

Pogo Books let children practice reading informational text while introducing them to nonfiction features such as headings, labels, sidebars, maps, and diagrams, as well as a table of contents, glossary, and index.

Carefully leveled text with a strong photo match offers early fluent readers the support they need to succeed.

Before Reading

- "Walk" through the book and point out the various nonfiction features. Ask the student what purpose each feature serves.
- Look at the glossary together. Read and discuss the words.

Read the Book

- Have the child read the book independently.
- Invite him or her to list questions that arise from reading.

After Reading

- Discuss the child's questions. Talk about how he or she might find answers to those questions.
- Prompt the child to think more. Ask: Slovakia is full of mountains. How do you think that affects life there?

Pogo Books are published by Jump!
5357 Penn Avenue South
Minneapolis, MN 55419
www.jumplibrary.com

Library of Congress Cataloging-in-Publication Data

Names: Spanier, Kristine, author.
Title: Slovakia / by Kristine Spanier, MLIS.
Description: Minneapolis, MN: Jump!, Inc., [2023]
Series: All around the world | Includes index.
Audience: Ages 7-10
Identifiers: LCCN 2022027142 (print)
LCCN 2022027143 (ebook)
ISBN 9798885242097 (hardcover)
ISBN 9798885242103 (paperback)
ISBN 9798885242110 (ebook)
Subjects: LCSH: Slovakia—Juvenile literature.
Classification: LCC DB2711 .S63 2023 (print)
LCC DB2711 (ebook)
DDC 943.73—dc23/eng/20220610
LC record available at https://lccn.loc.gov/2022027142
LC ebook record available at https://lccn.loc.gov/2022027143

Editor: Jenna Gleisner
Designer: Molly Ballanger

Photo Credits: Marcin Krzyzak/Shutterstock, cover; Martin Jancek/Getty, 1; Pixfiction/Shutterstock, 3; Tomas Hulik ARTpoint/Shutterstock, 4; saiko3p/Shutterstock, 5, 14-15; Fotokon/Shutterstock, 6-7; Rene Gabrielli/Shutterstock, 8; zedspider/Shutterstock, 8-9; Jaroslav Moravcik/Shutterstock, 10-11; Kaycco/iStock, 12; MICHAL CIZEK/AFP/Getty, 13; Branislav Cerven/Shutterstock, 16 (dumplings); Catto32/iStock, 16 (soup); Halfpoint/iStock, 17; Lubo Ivanko/Shutterstock, 18-19; Michal Knitl/Shutterstock, 20-21; RomanR/Shutterstock, 23.

Printed in the United States of America at Corporate Graphics in North Mankato, Minnesota.

TABLE OF CONTENTS

CHAPTER 1

LAND OF MOUNTAINS

Would you like to explore a castle? You can in Slovakia! Spiš Castle was built more than 900 years ago. It is one of the biggest castles in Europe.

Spiš Castle

Danube River

Slovakia is in Central Europe. It is **landlocked**. The Danube River flows along the southern border. Ships carry **goods** along this river.

Slovak Ore Mountains

Slovakia is full of mountain ranges. The Tatra Mountains are in the north. They create a natural border with Poland. The Slovak Ore Mountains are in the center of the country.

TAKE A LOOK!

What are the tallest peaks of some of Slovakia's major mountain ranges? Take a look!

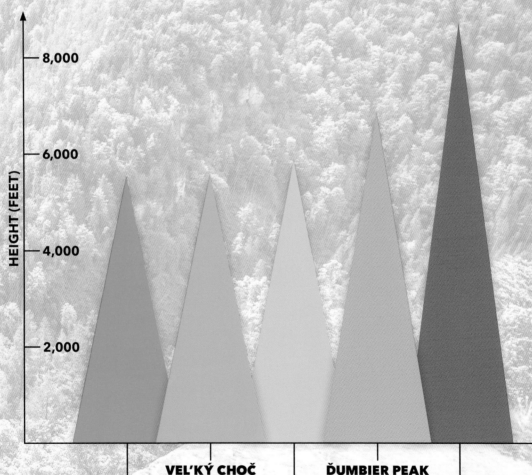

HEIGHT (FEET)

- 8,000
- 6,000
- 4,000
- 2,000

VEL'KÝ CHOČ
Chočské Vrchy Mountains
5,285 feet (1,611 meters)

ĎUMBIER PEAK
Low Tatra Mountains
6,703 feet (2,043 meters)

OSTREDOK
Vel'ká Fatra Mountains
5,236 feet (1,596 meters)

VEL'KY KRIVÁŇ
Malá Fatra Mountains
5,607 feet (1,709 meters)

GERLACHOVSKÝ PEAK
High Tatra Mountains
8,711 feet (2,655 meters)

Vlkolínec is a village in the Vel'ká Fatra Mountains. People have lived here for more than 650 years. Homes and barns from the 1700s are still here. In the past, the bell tower warned of fires and other dangers.

bell tower

Vlkolínec

Tatra chamois

The Tatra chamois got its name from the mountains. It is a kind of antelope. Bears, wolves, and lynx also make their homes in the mountains.

DID YOU KNOW?

Slovakia's national bird is the golden eagle. It nests in mountains and cliffs.

CHAPTER 2

SLOVAKIA'S GOVERNMENT

Slovakia and the Czech Republic used to be one country. It was called Czechoslovakia. Leaders agreed to split on January 1, 1993. This decision is celebrated every January 1. This day also marks the New Year. People can watch fireworks in Bratislava.

ballot

Bratislava is the **capital**. The president lives here. People can vote for the president when they turn 18.

People also vote for the Slovak National Council. This group makes laws. The government holds large events at Bratislava Castle.

WHAT DO YOU THINK?

Slovakia joined the **North Atlantic Treaty Organization (NATO)** in 2004. It joined the **European Union (EU)** that same year. Countries in these groups work together. They want to stay free. Do you think it is important for countries to be **independent**? Why or why not?

Bratislava
Castle

CHAPTER 3

....

DAILY LIFE

Slovakia's national dish is potato dumplings. These are covered in sheep's milk cheese. People also eat sauerkraut soup and potato pancakes. A pastry with nuts, apricots, and vanilla is a sweet treat!

potato dumplings

sauerkraut soup

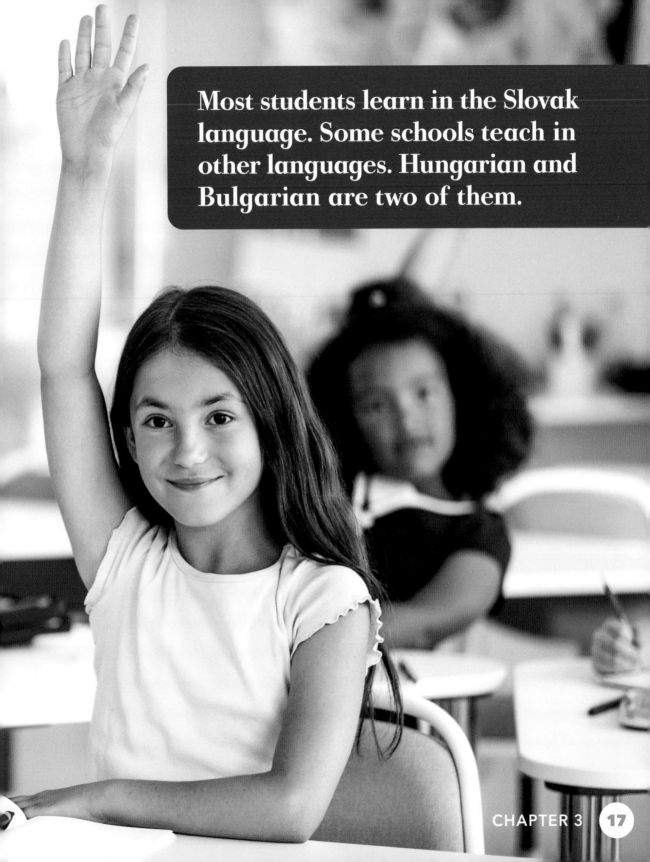

Most students learn in the Slovak language. Some schools teach in other languages. Hungarian and Bulgarian are two of them.

Ice hockey is a popular sport. People play it on frozen lakes in winter. People ski in the mountains. In summer, many play soccer.

The fujara was invented here. It is a long wooden flute. Some are more than six feet (1.8 m) long! **Shepherds** once played these instruments to pass the time with their sheep. Now they are played at **folk** festivals.

There is a lot to see and do in Slovakia. Do you want to visit?

WHAT DO YOU THINK?

Folk music is passed down from **generation** to generation. It tells stories about a country's history. Do you think it is important to remember history? Why or why not?

fujara ····▶

QUICK FACTS & TOOLS

SLOVAKIA

Location: Central Europe

Size: 18,932 square miles (49,034 square kilometers)

Population: 5,431,252 (2022 estimate)

Capital: Bratislava

Type of Government: parliamentary republic

Languages: Slovak (official), Hungarian, Czech

Exports: cars and vehicle parts, video displays, broadcasting equipment, tires, refined petroleum

Currency: euro

capital: A city where government leaders meet.

European Union (EU): A group of European countries that have joined together to encourage economic and political cooperation.

folk: Traditional and belonging to the common people in a region.

generation: All the people born around the same time.

goods: Things that are traded or sold.

independent: Free from a controlling authority.

landlocked: Not having any borders that touch the sea.

North Atlantic Treaty Organization (NATO): An organization of countries that have agreed to give each other military help. This group includes the United States, Canada, and some countries in Europe.

shepherds: People whose job is to herd, guard, and take care of sheep.

Slovakia's currency

INDEX

TO LEARN MORE

Finding more information is as easy as 1, 2, 3.

❶ Go to www.factsurfer.com

❷ Enter "Slovakia" into the search box.

❸ Choose your book to see a list of websites.

FACT SURFER